D0583535

LIVING GREEN

Green Transportation

WORLD
BOOK

a Scott Fetzer company
Chicago
www.worldbookonline.com

Editorial:

Editor in Chief: Paul A. Kobasa
Project Manager: Cassie Mayer
Writer: Robert N. Knight
Editor: Brian Johnson
Researcher: Mike Barr
Manager, Contracts & Compliance
  (Rights & Permissions): Loranne K. Shields
Indexer: David Pofelski

Graphics and Design:

Associate Director: Sandra M. Dyrlund
Manager: Tom Evans
Coordinator, Design Development
  and Production: Brenda B. Tropinski
Book design by: Don Di Sante
Senior Designer: Isaiah W. Sheppard, Jr.
Senior Cartographer: John Rejba

Pre-Press and Manufacturing:

Director: Carma Fazio
Manufacturing Manager: Steve Hueppchen
Production/Technology Manager: Anne Fritzinger

World Book, Inc.
233 N. Michigan Avenue
Chicago, IL 60601
U.S.A.

For information about other World Book publications, visit our Web site at **http://www.worldbookonline.com** or call **1-800-WORLDBK (967-5325)**.

For information about sales to schools and libraries, call **1-800-975-3250 (United States)**, or **1-800-837-5365 (Canada)**.

Library of Congress Cataloging-in-Publication Data

Green transportation.
   p. cm. -- (Living green)
   Includes index.
   Summary: "An overview of current efforts to reduce the environmental impact of various forms of transportation. Topics include biofuels, hybrid and battery-powered vehicles, fuel cell batteries, and solar technology. Features include fact boxes, glossary, activities, list of recommended reading and Web sites, and index"—Provided by publisher.
   ISBN 978-0-7166-1405-0
   1. Automobiles--Motors--Exhaust gas--Environmental aspects--Juvenile literature.
I. World Book, Inc.
TD886.5.G74 2008
629.04028'6—dc22
                    2008022796

Picture Acknowledgments:

Front Cover: © Andrew Woodley, Alamy Images
APAME Group/ELECTRAVIA/ACV Aero Service 51; © Graham Corney, Alamy Images 53; © Paul Glendell, Alamy Images 30; © Bert Klassen, Alamy Images 39; © Nic Miller, Organics Image Library/Alamy Images 1; © David Palmer, Alamy Images 41; AP/Wide World 16, 18, 20, 36, 43; © Peter Frischmuth from Peter Arnold, Inc. 44; Boeing 51; Brammo Motorsports 23; © Frances M. Roberts, Ambient Images/Digital Railroad 33; © Marcos Issa, Digital Railroad 22; © Cosmo Condina, Mira/Digital Railroad 56; © Colin Dutton, SIME/4Corners Images 24; © Karen Bleier, AFP/Getty Images 24; © Dylan Cross, AFP/Getty Images 45; © Popperfoto/Getty Images 9; © Mario Tama, Getty Images 38; © Granger Collection 8, 29; © David Gard, Times of Trenton/Newhouse News Service/Landov 21; © Marcos Brindicci, Reuters/Landov 31; © Masterfile 40; © Gary Gerovac, Masterfile 5; © R. Ian Lloyd, Masterfile 14; Michael Chia-Liang Lin, MIT Smart Cities group 25; Franco Vairani, MIT Smart Cities group 21; NOAA Great Lakes Environmental Research Laboratory 42; © Qilai Shen, Panos Pictures 10; Railpower 35; © Shutterstock 4, 5, 6, 13, 17, 26, 28, 32, 34, 37, 46, 48, 49, 54, 55, 57, 59; © age fotostock/SuperStock 27; © Culver Pictures/SuperStock 12; © Photononstop/SuperStock 58; Toyota Motor Sales, U.S.A., Inc. 19, 52; Staff Sgt. Bennie J. Davis III, U.S. Air Force 50; © Gamma/Eyedea/ZUMA Press 16; © Yusnirsyah Sirin, JiwaFoto/ZUMA Press 15.

All maps and illustrations are the exclusive property of World Book, Inc.

Living Green
Set ISBN: 978-0-7166-1400-5
Printed in China
2 3 4 5 6 13 12 11 10 09

Table of Contents

Some words in the text appear in bold, **like this.** They are defined in the glossary on pages 60-61. Words are bolded at the first use in each section.

Transportation: A Basic Human Need

Section Summary

Transportation includes all the ways people and goods move about the world. Modern transportation has dramatically changed the way we live, but this mobility comes at great cost to the environment.

Most forms of transportation use fuel made from petroleum (oil), a resource that is in limited supply and will eventually run out. Burning fuel made from petroleum is one of the leading causes of pollution.

Burning petroleum also releases carbon dioxide gas. The build-up of carbon dioxide in the atmosphere causes global warming. Reducing transportation's environmental impact is vital to preserving Earth.

A car takes a California family across the United States to visit the Maine coast. A jet whisks vacationers from a January deep-freeze in Canada to a sunny Caribbean island. A massive ship, bigger than a warehouse, travels across the ocean carrying millions of gallons of **crude oil.**

Thousands of commercial airplanes crisscross the globe every day.

All of these scenes are examples of transportation. Transportation is any means of moving people or goods. Without rapid transportation, our modern civilization would come to a screeching halt. Many uses of transportation are familiar to us—cars to drive to school or work, passenger trains to take medium-distance trips, airplanes to take long-distance trips. Most of us, however, rarely think about "behind-the-scenes" transportation that supports our way of life. For example, all of the food we buy in grocery stores has been shipped from somewhere. The natural gas or oil that heats many of our homes may have traveled underground through pipelines. Mail services rely on many forms of transportation, including trucks and airplanes.

The costs of transportation

Cargo ships, such as this one, transport large volumes of goods around the world.

All transportation requires energy, and energy is an expensive commodity (good) in our modern world. For the past century, much of the world's activities have run on the energy in **petroleum** (also called oil), coal, and natural gas. These fuels are called **fossil fuels.** Fossil fuels come from underground deposits that were formed millions of years ago from the remains of plants and animals. Today, we know that supplies of fossil fuels are dwindling and will eventually run out. Thus, they are described as **nonrenewable resources.** When they are gone, they will be gone forever. Because people around the world are using fossil fuels more quickly than new supplies are becoming available, these fuels are becoming more and more expensive.

Another cost of using fossil fuels is the pollution they release. Pollution is dirt and waste that can harm living things and the environment. Over time, pollution can overwhelm natural cycles that keep Earth clean and healthy.

Oil, coal, and natural gas must be burned to release their energy. Burning, or **combustion,** is a chemical reaction in which oxygen from the air combines chemically with such a fuel as wood, oil, or coal. The chemical reaction gives off energy in the form of light and heat. It also gives off **carbon dioxide** (a colorless, odorless gas), water vapor, and smaller amounts of other substances.

Automobiles burn huge amounts of fossil fuels, releasing much pollution.

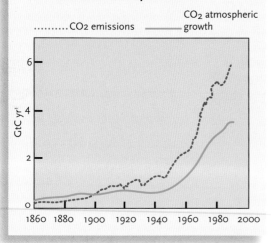

Carbon dioxide build-up over time

········ CO2 emissions ———— CO2 atmospheric growth

The chart above compares the annual growth rate of carbon dioxide in the atmosphere (green line) to the annual rate of emissions released by human activities (red line).

Such vehicles as motorcycles release carbon dioxide gas and other harmful pollutants.

Carbon dioxide

The gas carbon dioxide, a major product of combustion, does not ordinarily harm living things directly. However, so much carbon dioxide has been released into the air by human activities that it is now seriously affecting the natural balance of gases in Earth's atmosphere. Carbon dioxide is a key component of air because it helps **regulate** Earth's temperature by holding some of the sun's heat within the atmosphere. This process is called the **greenhouse effect**, and it is crucial for keeping Earth warm. But as carbon dioxide builds up in the atmosphere, it traps more and more heat. Because it helps drive the greenhouse effect, carbon dioxide is called a **greenhouse gas**. It is not the only greenhouse gas in the atmosphere, but it is the most abundant one.

Global warming

The build-up of carbon dioxide is one of the main causes of **global warming.** The surface temperature of Earth has been rising over the past century, and most scientists believe that these rising temperatures are due mainly to human activities, such as the burning of fossil fuels.

Transportation is not the only area of human activity responsible for pouring carbon dioxide into the atmosphere. Other activities, such as manufacturing (making goods in factories), generating electric power in power plants, and heating buildings also release carbon dioxide. However, transportation is one of the main ways people release carbon dioxide, and the need for it continues to grow. Any plan for turning toward a greener way of living must address people's transportation needs.

Another "Transportation Revolution"

Modern transportation has transformed human societies, but it has also contributed to pollution problems on a scale that people never experienced or even imagined before 1800. For most of human history, people moved about solely by their own human power, by the power of animals, or by the power of wind. No motorized transportation of any kind was developed for widespread practical use before about 1800. Historians coined the phrase "Transportation Revolution" to describe the rapid improvements in transportation that began in the 1800's.

We may be entering a new revolution in transportation today. In order to stop the rapid build-up of carbon dioxide and other **pollutants** in our atmosphere, engineers and scientists are working hard to develop new transportation technologies that will be far less polluting. Some new modes of transportation may cause little or no pollution at all. Thirty years from now, people may look back at our era and be amazed that we used such inefficient, polluting machines.

Changes in transportation have been recent and quite rapid when compared to the entire history of civilization.

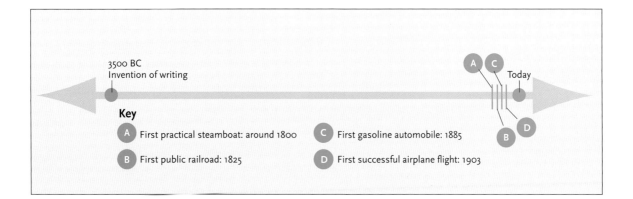

3500 BC
Invention of writing

Today

Key

A First practical steamboat: around 1800

B First public railroad: 1825

C First gasoline automobile: 1885

D First successful airplane flight: 1903

Automobiles

Section Summary

Automobiles are a major source of pollution. Most automobiles run on gasoline fuel made from petroleum. Burning gasoline releases carbon dioxide gas, along with other pollutants.

Scientists and automakers are working to develop automobiles that produce less pollution. Electric and hybrid automobiles are becoming more advanced and affordable. These vehicles are becoming increasingly popular as technologies improve and fuel costs continue to rise.

Scientists are also developing alternative fuels that cause less pollution than fossil fuels. Some vehicles already use biofuels (fuels made from plants).

The Model T Ford, first sold in 1908, was one of first affordable cars sold in the United States.

One of the most widespread forms of transportation today is the personal car, or automobile. The automobile is at the front and center of environmental concerns about transportation. To understand why, it is necessary to understand the **internal-combustion engine**, the source of power in most cars.

Internal-combustion engines burn a mixture of air and fuel inside closed cylinders. As the fuel burns, it produces expanding gases that force objects called pistons to move inside each cylinder. Connecting rods transmit this power to a shaft called the crankshaft, which converts the pistons' up-and-down movement into rotary (circular) movement. This motion is then transmitted to the wheels that move the car.

The engines of most cars operate on a four-stroke cycle. In this cycle, pistons within a cylinder go down-up-down-up, turning the crankshaft two revolutions (movements that make a complete circle). At the end of each cycle, burned gases, called **exhaust**, are pushed out of the cylinder and into a pipe that releases the gases.

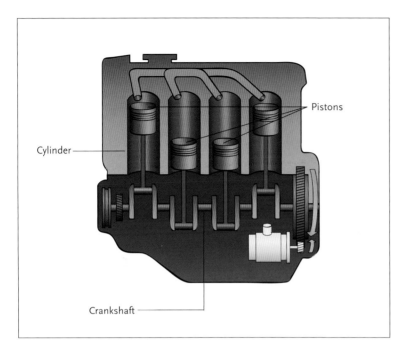

An internal-combustion
engine burns fuel to drive
pistons that turn a crankshaft.

A German engineer named Gottlieb
Daimler (1834–1900) developed the
first truly modern internal-combustion
engine. Although Daimler did not in-
vent the idea of the internal-combustion engine, he and his partner,
Wilhelm Maybach, developed a practical form of the device at their work-
shop in Stuttgart, Germany, in 1885.
That same year, Daimler attached an
engine to a bicycle, creating the world's
first motorcycle.

In 1889, Daimler and Maybach introduced their first truly integrated automobile. Their work set the foundation
for the Daimler-Benz Company, which
became one of the leading automobile
manufacturers in the world.

Ingenious—and inefficient

The internal combustion engine is truly an ingenious device. It
became the core component of hundreds of millions of automobiles manufactured within the past century. However, the internal-combustion engine is also extremely inefficient.

Fuel efficiency in cars and other modes of transportation re-
lates to the engine's ability to create power with the least amount
of wasted energy. In an efficient machine, most of the energy is
converted into power that can be used to do a job. However, the
internal-combustion engines typically used in cars achieve an efficiency of only about 20 to 25 percent, meaning that about three-
quarters of the energy is wasted. Almost all of this wasted energy
is converted into heat. The reason for heat conversion is that an
internal-combustion engine has many rapidly moving parts. All
of that movement causes friction, which generates heat.

Automobiles   9

AUTOMOBILE POLLUTION

Internal-combustion engines produce power by burning a **fossil fuel**, such as gasoline, in **combustion** chambers. This process produces airborne waste products, called **emissions**, which are released through the exhaust system into the air.

Automobile emissions include **carbon dioxide**, the main cause of **global warming**. Other substances in automobile emissions include carbon monoxide, hydrocarbons, nitrogen oxides, volatile organic compounds (VOC's), and **particulates**. The chart on this page describes these substances and their effects on living things or the environment in general.

Chemical mischief-makers

Each automobile on the road fills the air with a variety of pollutants.

Automobile emissions can combine with other substances in the air to form different types of pollution. For example, nitrogen oxides combine with water vapor and sulfur dioxide, a **pollutant** re-

Pollutants in Automobile Exhaust		
Pollutant	Description	Environmental or health threat
Carbon dioxide	Colorless, odorless gas; main product of combustion	Traps the sun's heat, causing global warming
Carbon monoxide	Poisonous, odorless, colorless gas	Extremely harmful to living things
Gaseous hydrocarbons	Complex molecules released because of incomplete combustion	Contribute to the formation of smog in cities
Nitrogen oxides	Compounds of nitrogen and oxygen, the two most abundant gases in air, formed in the presence of high heat	Contribute to the formation of smog and acid rain
Volatile organic compounds (VOC's)	Carbon-containing compounds that produce vapors at room temperature	Harmful to living things
Particulates	Very fine pieces of solid material that float freely in air; also called soot	Contain lead, a particulate that is extremely harmful to living things

leased by coal-burning power plants. Together, these substances become **acid rain**. Acid rain has seriously damaged bodies of water, forests, and stone structures in many parts of the world.

Smog is a type of air pollution that forms when exhaust gases combine chemically in the presence of sunlight. One component of smog is a form of oxygen called **ozone**, a sharp-smelling gas that can damage the lungs. Smog becomes especially concentrated in cities, creating unhealthy breathing conditions.

The catalytic converter

Modern cars contain a device called the **catalytic converter** that helps reduce the number of pollutants given off by an internal-combustion engine. The design of the catalytic converter is based on the chemical action of certain catalysts (substances that speed chemical reactions), which help convert pollutants to less harmful or even harmless substances.

Burned gases from the engine flow through the boxlike catalytic converter, which is installed in a vehicle's exhaust system. The inside of the catalytic converter consists of tiny, honeycomblike passages that are coated with thin layers of such metals as platinum, palladium, and rhodium. These metals, which do not corrode easily, serve as the catalysts. As the exhaust gases flow through the coated passages, chemical reactions take place that convert pollutants into harmless substances.

The catalytic converter does not eliminate the problem of air pollution by cars. However, it does eliminate or reduce some of the more harmful pollutants. Cars with catalytic converters came widely into use in the United States in 1975.

Catalytic converters use catalysts to convert pollutants into harmless substances.

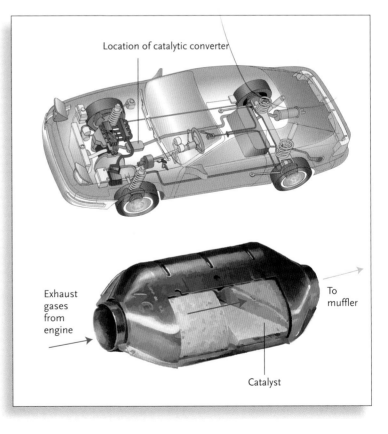

Location of catalytic converter

Exhaust gases from engine

To muffler

Catalyst

Bigger is not better

Fuel economy is a measurement of how many miles (or kilometers) a vehicle can drive for every gallon (or liter) of fuel it burns. Weight is a significant factor in fuel economy and in rates of pollution. The larger and heavier a vehicle is, the more fuel it needs to burn for power. As a result, larger and heavier vehicles release more pollutants into the air.

Traditionally, many U.S. drivers have favored large automobiles. In the years after World War II (1939–1945), U.S. automakers offered big, heavy cars to an eager public. From the early 1980's onward, many automakers produced large numbers of **sport utility vehicles (SUV's).** They also produced a wider variety of pickup trucks and other small trucks. By the year 2000, nearly one-quarter of all new automobiles sold by U.S. automakers were SUV's.

An SUV is a passenger vehicle that combines the features of a station wagon and a truck. An SUV is taller and larger than a normal car. It is officially classified by federal agencies as a "light truck." Like a standard truck, an SUV features elevated driver seating and extra ground clearance. Most SUV's, as well as vans and pickup trucks, are heavier than most cars. Because the U.S. federal government **regulates** cars differently than SUV's, vans, and pickup trucks, these heavier automobiles are permitted to give off more pollutants than cars.

Automakers in the United States have traditionally built large, heavy vehicles, such as those made in the 1940's.

Danger in numbers

In the early years of the automobile era, few car users thought about air pollution. If they did, they assumed that the atmosphere would take care of itself. Today, however, the number of automobiles on Earth is enormous. There is one automobile for every seven people on the planet—about 900 million cars in all. Some experts believe that by 2020, there will be 1.2 billion automobiles on Earth. Even that estimate may be low, because the world's two most populous countries, China and India, are industrializing rapidly. Their populations are creating tremendous demand for more automobiles.

Analysts with the Sierra Club, an environmental organization in the United States and Canada, estimate that the average car gives off more than 70 tons (64 metric tons) of carbon dioxide emissions over its lifetime. An SUV gives off more than 100 tons (91 metric tons) of carbon dioxide over its lifetime. Given the number of cars in the world, this rate of pollution is a serious threat to the health of our planet.

Many experts believe that scientists, engineers, and car manufacturing companies will have to redesign cars to make them far less polluting. That work is already in progress. In the future, it is likely that automobile designers will be inspired by the motto, "less is more."

Creating smaller, lighter cars that are safe and perform well is one of the major challenges of the 21st century.

The roads in such large cities as Bangkok, Thailand, are often congested with commuter traffic.

SUFFERING CITIES

The 900 million cars on Earth today are not evenly distributed around the globe. Like the world's people, they are highly concentrated in cities. Since the mid-1900's, the world has become rapidly more **urban** (city-dwelling). In 1975, only about a third of the world's people lived in urban areas. By 2008, about half were living in such places. (An urban area is defined as a built-up area in or adjacent to a city or town.)

As cities in the United States and other parts of the world have spread out into vast suburban regions, the number of cars in cities has multiplied many times over. This multitude of automobiles has concentrated air pollution, particularly smog, more and more in urban areas.

One factor that intensifies air pollution from cars is traffic **congestion.** Many large cities have so many cars on the road at **rush hour** (times of the day when workers are driving to work or home from work) that the cars move very slowly or sometimes just sit in place—with their motors running. A 2005 study of the amount of fuel wasted in traffic congestion showed that in more than 400 cities across the United States, each driver wasted an average of 26 gallons (98 liters) of gasoline during that single year. This added up to a total of 2.9 billion gallons (10.9 billion liters) of fuel wasted for the year—enough to fill the fuel tanks of 290,000 trucks.

This map shows the location of the largest developing megalopolis (continuous metropolitan area) in the United States and the major expressways that connect its cities.

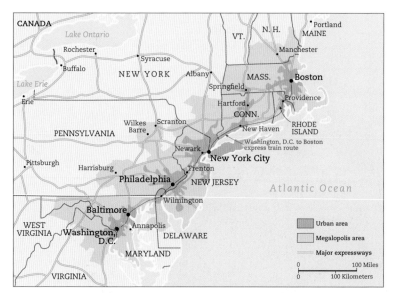

The Los Angeles story

Los Angeles was perhaps the world's first city to experience air pollution problems due mainly to automobiles. By the 1940's, residents were beginning to take note of smoggy days (which they called "gas attacks"). By the 1950's and 1960's, smog in Los Angeles had become a major problem.

In the 1960's, 1970's, and 1980's, local governments and the California state government took action. These governments regulated the amount of pollution that factories, power plants, cars, trucks, buses, and other polluters could release. They also encouraged workers in offices to carpool. Los Angeles has succeeded in sharply reducing its air pollution. However, it was still rated as the most polluted city in the United States in a study conducted in 2007.

Los Angeles officials and citizens are fighting pollution against strong odds. The city's population has nearly doubled in size since the 1950's. In fact, Los Angeles has become one of the great **megacities** of the modern world. A megacity is defined as an urban area with 10 million or more residents. The more people flock to cities, the worse the pollution becomes. The pollution problems of Los Angeles are worsened by the fact that the number of automobiles in the urban area has surpassed the increase in population. Los Angeles is often described as the first "car city," and historically, public transportation was not a high priority.

A CLOSER LOOK
Megacity Jakarta

Jakarta, the capital city of Indonesia, has experienced explosive growth in the past 25 years. The entire urban area, including suburbs, has a population of around 14 million. In 2005, the city's transport agency estimated that 7 million gasoline engines were polluting Jakarta's air every day.

All of this air pollution seriously affects the health of Jakarta's citizens. According to statistics reported in 2000, Jakarta had the second-highest number of deaths in the world due to air pollution. Indonesian elected officials are beginning to study the problem of pollution and how to reduce it.

Jakarta, Indonesia

BIOFUELS

Biofuels may offer a less polluting way to fuel vehicles than **petroleum**-based gasoline. These liquid fuels are made from living things or their products, and their use is growing substantially in the United States and other countries.

Ethanol, a kind of alcohol made from corn, sugar cane, or other plants, is a type of biofuel that is typically mixed with gasoline to power cars. Much of the gasoline used in the United States is a blend of 10 percent ethanol and 90 percent gasoline. E-85 cars run on 85 percent ethanol and 15 percent gasoline. To run on E-85, cars must be manufactured and sold as E-85 cars, or their engines must be modified. These cars also must find gas stations that sell the E-85 blend.

Advantages of biofuels

Unlike petroleum-based fuels, most biofuels are made from plants, which are a **renewable resource.** Using such fuels may help **conserve** our limited supply of oil, which is a **nonrenewable resource.** Biofuels also give off fewer harmful pollutants than petroleum-based fuels. Burning biofuels does release carbon dioxide, but it releases only the amount of carbon dioxide that the crops absorbed during their lifetime. In other words, biofuels are part of a natural **carbon cycle** that does not substantially harm Earth. Plants take in carbon while alive and release it when burned, causing no long-term change in the amount of carbon dioxide in the atmosphere. By contrast, the carbon dioxide in fossil fuels would ordinarily remain locked away deep inside Earth. Burning fossil fuels disrupts the carbon cycle by adding to the overall amount of carbon dioxide in the atmosphere. Earth may require millions of years to lock away this carbon dioxide again.

Scientists are researching new and better ways to turn plants into biofuel.

Many U.S. citizens believe that biofuels may reduce the country's dependence on petroleum, which must be imported from other countries.

Disadvantages of biofuels

Some experts argue that biofuels may cause more environmental damage than petroleum-based fuels. For example, if biofuels were to become a significant source of fuel, more land would be cleared in order to grow enough crops to meet the demand. Trees and other plants absorb carbon dioxide, so their destruction disrupts Earth's natural ability to remove carbon dioxide from the atmosphere. In addition, the growth of corn, one of the main crops used to make ethanol, requires large amounts of **herbicides** and chemical **fertilizers**. These substances are typically made from fossil fuels. They can also cause air and water pollution.

Though burning biofuels releases only the carbon dioxide that biofuel crops absorbed prior to harvesting, making biofuel can release large amounts of additional carbon dioxide. For example, farmers may use large amounts of fossil fuels to produce the crops used to make biofuels. It is thus possible to burn more fossil fuels in producing biofuel than the biofuel actually saves. This is a particular concern with corn, one of the main crops used to make biofuel. Corn is not dense with energy, so a lot of it must be used in order to make biofuel.

A need for new technologies

Scientists are currently researching ways to make more **sustainable** biofuels. One solution may be to make ethanol from **cellulose,** a plant material consisting of tightly bound chains of sugar molecules. Researchers are looking for inexpensive ways to break down cellulose into simple sugars that can be easily converted into ethanol. Then, instead of cultivating corn, energy farmers could raise such plants as switchgrass or buffalo grass to make ethanol. These grasses can grow on land that is unsuitable for food crops. They also require less energy to grow.

Most scientists and government officials agree that biofuels hold much promise as an alternative energy source. However, more research is needed in order to avoid causing unintentional harm to the environment— and to the world's people.

In many countries, crops that were once grown for food are now being grown for fuel. In 2006, 14 percent of all corn grown in the United States went to biofuel production. The U.S. Department of Agriculture predicts that by 2016, the percentage will double. Some experts warn that the increased use of grains for fuel may lead to higher food prices. In 2008, food prices around the world rose sharply, leading to riots in some countries. Experts believe many factors caused high food prices, from increased demand for food in such rapidly developing countries as India to droughts where these crops are normally grown. The increased use of crops for biofuels was also cited as a significant factor.

A biofuel plant and cornfields

ELECTRIC CARS AND HYBRIDS

Battery-powered cars have been around for a long time. Until recently, however, they have never been very practical. Their batteries gave out quickly and had to be recharged after a limited number of miles.

The Tesla Roadster is an all-electric sports car that began production in 2008.

Electric cars

Today, people are taking a second look at electric cars, also called battery-powered cars. Researchers have developed stronger, longer-lasting batteries. They have also learned how to build strong, safe, light-weight car bodies. Electric cars create no exhaust, and they run quietly.

One of the most promising technologies in electric cars today is the lithium-ion battery. An electric car typically has a number of batteries in a battery pack. However, the weight of all these batteries is a limiting factor. Because the lithium-ion battery is lighter than other similar batteries, a car can reasonably house enough of these batteries to give it a range of 300 miles (483 kilometers) before it needs to be plugged in and recharged.

Electric cars are not truly pollution-free because they have to be plugged into electrical outlets in order to recharge their batteries. Electric cars will not be pollution-free until power plants are also pollution-free. However, electric cars make far more efficient use of energy than do traditional cars. Also, producing electric power at power plants is much less polluting than burning fossil fuels in numerous internal-combustion engines. As a result, electric cars would represent a huge advance in reducing pollution.

Hybrid cars

Hybrid cars use both electric power and a small gasoline engine. This arrangement gives a hybrid car several advantages. Because the gasoline engine can recharge the batteries, the hybrid's range is equivalent to that of a standard gasoline-powered car. Also, the hybrid car can obtain quick bursts of power from the gasoline engine when the driver needs to "step on it"—for example, when merging into fast-moving expressway traffic.

The hybrid power system is ingenious and complex. Sensors and computers shift the gasoline engine from power mode (actually running the car) to recharge mode (recharging the batteries). The power system also captures energy from braking to recharge the battery in a process that is called **regenerative braking**.

A variation on the standard hybrid is the plug-in hybrid. This type of car has a plug-in attachment to recharge the battery. However, the gasoline engine is still available if the charge runs low. Plug-in hybrids are even more efficient than ordinary hybrids.

Pros and cons of hybrids

The hybrid car uses far less gasoline than standard cars, but it remains dependent on petroleum production. Unlike the electric car, it does produce exhaust. And because of its complexity, a hybrid car is more expensive than a traditional gasoline-powered car. Still, if a substantial number of drivers switched from standard cars to hybrid cars, the amount of air pollution in urban areas would decrease significantly.

A CLOSER LOOK
Regenerative Braking
When the driver presses the brake in a standard car, the brake system causes a pad to be pressed against the wheel assembly. This action creates friction that slows the car. However, it also releases energy in the form of heat. This heat is wasted energy—it does no useful work.

At high speeds, a hybrid car uses traditional braking. However, in stop-and-go traffic, pressing the brakes causes the electric motor to reverse direction, which slows or stops the car. In its reverse mode, the electric motor recharges the battery, so stopping and starting in city traffic actually saves energy. By contrast, this type of driving in a standard gasoline car wastes energy and increases emissions.

The Toyota Prius is a popular hybrid car. It contains a display that monitors energy use.

ALTERNATIVE VEHICLES

Researchers today are experimenting with a number of different energy-producing systems that could power cars. One of the most promising is the hydrogen **fuel cell**.

Fuel cells

A fuel cell causes a chemical reaction and converts chemical energy into electric power. In this way, it is similar to a battery. However, in a fuel cell, the chemicals necessary for the reaction are supplied to the cell from the outside.

A common fuel cell is the hydrogen fuel cell. This device receives hydrogen gas from a pressurized fuel tank in the car and draws oxygen from the air around the car. Inside the fuel cell, the oxygen and hydrogen are combined chemically in a way that frees **electrons** (tiny parts of atoms) to produce an electric current. The reaction produces no exhaust and no pollutants. The only waste product is water.

Car companies have already manufactured cars that are powered by fuel cells, though the technology is still evolving. One of the chief problems with fuel-cell technology is how to create a reasonably priced supply of hydrogen and get it to fuel pumps so drivers can use it. Some companies have developed home-energy stations, which transform natural gas into pure hydrogen gas that can replenish a fuel cell. Other companies are developing special panels that would use water and energy from the sun to generate hydrogen. It remains to be seen, however, if this technology can become inexpensive enough to be used widely.

Many companies have developed fuel-cell cars, but none is yet widely available.

Batteries and fuel cells each offer advantages and disadvantages.

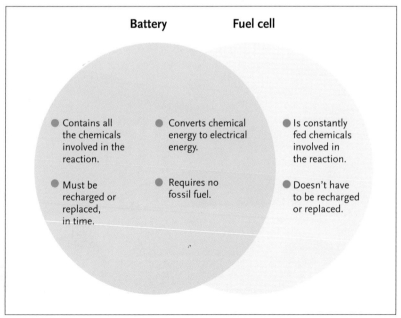

Battery		Fuel cell
● Contains all the chemicals involved in the reaction.	● Converts chemical energy to electrical energy.	● Is constantly fed chemicals involved in the reaction.
● Must be recharged or replaced, in time.	● Requires no fossil fuel.	● Doesn't have to be recharged or replaced.

Natural gas vehicles

Some service stations have natural gas pumps for NGV's.

Since the 1990's, some auto-manufacturing companies have produced a limited number of **natural gas vehicles (NGV's)**. These cars are powered by an internal-combustion engine, but the engine runs on natural gas instead of gasoline. Although burning natural gas does produce some pollution, it burns much more cleanly than gasoline.

Energy experts believe that natural gas may be more abundant underground in the United States than petroleum. Also, natural gas has consistently been cheaper at the pump than gasoline since energy prices began to climb steeply after 2000.

One major drawback of NGV's is that natural gas has not caught on in a big way, so there are few natural gas filling stations. However, drivers of NGV vehicles can purchase a home-refilling unit that taps into the standard natural gas feed that homeowners use for heating and cooking. The refilling unit takes some time to fill the car's storage tank, so using it is rather like plugging in an electric car overnight.

Natural gas is an improvement over gasoline, but it is far from ideal. An NGV vehicle does give off some exhaust, and it also releases carbon dioxide into the atmosphere.

A CLOSER LOOK
MIT's "City Car"

Researchers at the Massachusetts Institute of Technology (MIT) are working to develop the "City Car," a small, two-passenger, all-electric car that is designed to be "stackable." City cars can stack into one another like grocery carts in a store. When the cars are stacked at designated charging stations, their batteries recharge.

The City Car is designed for people who need connecting transportation between two points, such as a train station and a central downtown location. People could take a car off the stack, drive it to the destination, and then put it back on a stack there for another person to use. The developers compare this usage to borrowing a luggage cart at the airport and then dropping it off at a designated place.

Motorcycles

Section Summary

Motorcycles are used for personal transportation in many parts of the world. In some cities, motorcycles are greater polluters than automobiles.

Engineers have sought ways to reduce motorcycles' environmental impact. Some motorcycles now run on biofuels, which release fewer pollutants than gasoline-powered motorcycles.

Smaller, lighter motorcycles, such as electric bikes, motor scooters, and personal transporters are also less polluting than standard motorcycles.

A motorcycle is any powered two- or three-wheeled vehicle. Traditionally, motorcycles have been powered by gasoline-fueled **internal-combustion engines.** Many smaller and older motorcycles use a two-stroke engine rather than the four-stroke engine common in cars. In a two-stroke engine, the pistons go up and down one time per cycle (rather than two times, as in a four-stroke engine). The two-stroke engine releases more **pollutants** than the four-stroke engine. Also, because motorcycles' **emissions** have not been **regulated** by governments to the extent that cars' emissions have, motorcycles are up to three times more polluting than cars.

In São Paulo, Brazil, the number of motorcycles has doubled in recent years.

In the United States, many people think of cars as the chief polluters among vehicles. However, in many parts of the world, the motorcycle is an equal or greater contributor to pollution. In São Paulo, Brazil—one of the world's largest **megacities**—5 million cars and 1 million motorcycles compete on city streets. In Delhi, India—another megacity—there are about 3 motorcycles for every car. In Kano, Nigeria, a city of about 3 million people, 2 million motorcycles take to the streets during **rush hour,** pouring out **exhaust** and creating **smog.**

It is clear that motorcycles will continue to be an important mode of personal transportation. Motorcycles are lighter, more compact, and cheaper than cars. For many of the world's people, motorcycles are the only affordable option for powered, personal transportation.

Going green with battery power

Researchers and manufacturers have begun to consider green alternatives to the world's highly polluting fleet of motorcycles. One option is powering motorcycles with batteries to achieve a **zero emissions vehicle (ZEV)**. Such vehicles are now available to consumers, but they are more expensive than standard gasoline-powered motorcycles. Like a battery-powered car, a ZEV motorcycle must be plugged in to recharge—typically for three hours or more. Industry experts expect that prices for ZEV's will come down as consumer demand increases and technological advances improve performance.

Biodiesel

In 2007, a group of engineering students at the University of Adelaide in Australia built a **biodiesel** motorcycle, which they dubbed the "BioBike." Biodiesel is a type of **biofuel** made from soybeans or other oil-producing plants. The engineering students demonstrated the vehicle by entering it into a competition and driving it across the Australian continent from Darwin in the north to Adelaide in the south, a distance of about 1,900 miles (3,000 kilometers). The Bio-Bike achieved a **fuel efficiency** rating of about 100 miles per gallon (43 kilometers per liter).

Another group of engineering students from the University of Adelaide entered their "Eco Trike" in the same competition. This three-wheeled motorcycle runs entirely on canola oil. Energy experts said that these biofuel-powered motorcycles demonstrated that motorcycle development and production could shift from internal-combustion power to cleaner technologies.

Electric motorcycles are emissions-free.

MOTORCYCLE ALTERNATIVES

Today, people often choose lighter, less powerful two-wheeled or three-wheeled vehicles. These options include the following:

- Motor scooter: a small, lightweight motorcycle with a step-through frame, flat floorboard for the rider's feet, and automatic transmission.
- Electric bicycle: a pedal bicycle assisted by a motor, typically powered by batteries.
- Personal transporter, or PT: a simplified motorized scooter on which riders stand. The machine maintains rider balance by means of a complex, computerized **gyroscope** system.

The Segway is a popular, electrically powered personal transporter.

Motor scooters

Motor scooters represent a popular variation on the motorcycle. They are lighter weight and easier to drive than a motorcycle. Almost all newer models have easy-to-use automatic transmissions.

The classic motor scooter is the Vespa ("wasp" in Italian), first manufactured in 1946 by Piaggio, an Italian company. Since that time, many improvements have been made to the motor scooter, but most scooters are still powered by an internal-combustion engine. As with other motorcycles, four-stroke engines in motorcycles are less polluting than two-stroke engines.

Some rechargeable, battery-powered scooters are available, and researchers are working to develop **hybrid** scooters. Like hybrid cars, these scooters would run on alternate powering from a paired electric motor and gasoline engine.

The Vespa is a popular Italian motor scooter.

Electric bicycles

Electric bicycles merge motorized power with pedals and a fairly standard bike frame. Some electric bicycles allow riders to use the bike either in powered or nonpowered mode (as a regular pedaled bicycle). Others use sensors and computer technology to automatically assist pedaling when needed. These types of electric bikes supply extra power when the bicyclist is climbing a hill, for example.

A modern electric bicycle is likely to have a range of 50 miles (80 kilometers) or more before needing a recharge. However, like other electric vehicles, electric bicycles must be plugged in for some time before their batteries recharge. An electric bicycle is also more expensive and heavier than a standard bicycle.

Personal transporters

Personal transporters, or PT's, were introduced to the marketplace in 2002 by the Segway company. The PT rider stands on the platform at the base of the scooter and holds onto handlebars. He or she moves the scooter by leaning in a particular direction. Although the vehicle looks like it would easily topple over, a computerized system of gyroscopes keeps the rider upright at all times.

The PT can travel up to 24 miles (38 kilometers) on a single charge and travel at a top speed of around 12 miles per hour (19 kilometers per hour). A number of U.S. city police departments have purchased PT's to bolster personal mobility of police officers. The U.S. Department of Defense is also funding research into how modified Segways might be used on the battlefield or in support roles removed from combat.

The greenest of them all— the bicycle

Of course, the greenest two-wheeled vehicle on the road remains the bicycle. People around the world commute by bike. Bicycles provide a pollution-free mode of transportation that also helps people stay fit. Large cities in Europe, Canada, and the United States provide bike lanes for cyclists to ride alongside cars.

A CLOSER LOOK
MIT's RoboScooter

Researchers at the Massachusetts Institute of Technology (MIT) have developed a prototype (early version) of a lightweight electric motor scooter—that folds up! Unlike other battery-powered scooters, the RoboScooter has electric motors in its wheels. This design allows the vehicle's operating system to be much less complex than those of other motorized bikes.

The RoboScooter is designed to be "green" and easy to use on city streets. When folded up, it can be wheeled along like a suitcase on wheels. People who need quick, inexpensive, easy transport between two points in a city would use a credit card to remove a RoboScooter from a rack, ride it to the destination, and then fold it up again to put back on a rack for someone else to use.

Trucks

Section Summary

Trucks are often used to transport goods from place to place. Trucks run on diesel, a type of fuel that releases more harmful pollutants than gasoline. Trucks need to be large and powerful enough to carry heavy loads, so they use lots of fuel. Because of this, trucks are major contributors to air pollution.

Some trucks now run on biodiesel, a fuel which can be made from oil-bearing plants. This type of fuel releases fewer pollutants than diesel.

A truck is a type of motor vehicle used to carry **freight** (any goods that must be transported). Trucks come in many sizes and shapes, and they carry a wide variety of goods. Our way of life would be impossible without trucks. They transport nearly everything we eat, wear, and use. Around 15.5 million trucks operate in the United States and make up a critical part of the transportation system.

Many trucks transport freight that must be transferred from one form of transportation to another. For example, a ship docks at a port. Cranes at the port remove containers from the ship and load them onto a truck. The truck then drives to a distribution center in another city and unloads the containers.

Because so much freight is shipped by truck, truck traffic has led to **congestion** on interstate highways and in cities. Also, trucks traditionally have been major contributors to **smog** and other forms of air pollution. Trucks need to be large and powerful enough to carry heavy loads of freight, so they use lots of fuel. In a typical year, U.S. trucking industries use about 13 percent of all transportation fuel used in the United States.

Despite its drawbacks, trucking is essential in the United

> **Trucks play a crucial role in transportation systems, but they use large amounts of polluting fossil fuels.**

States and world economies. It is also an important employer. There are about 3.3 million truck drivers in the United States and more than a 250,000 truck drivers in Canada.

There are a number of styles and sizes of trucks. The chart below presents some of the most common types.

Trucks carry containers unloaded from ships to distribution centers.

Types of Trucks

Pickup truck
The smallest truck, often used as a personal vehicle. Weighs between 5,000 pounds (2,270 kilograms) and 14,000 pounds (6,356 kilograms).

Panel truck
A small, fully enclosed truck. Example: Rental trucks for moving loads.

Flatbed truck
Consists of a closed cab in front of a flat, open platform for loading cargo. Can carry extremely heavy loads, such as steel beams. Maximum weight: 80,000 pounds (36,320 kilograms).*

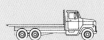

Tank truck
Consists of a closed cab in front of a large tank for carrying liquids such as gasoline, **ethanol,** or milk. Maximum weight: 80,000 pounds (36,320 kilograms).

Tractor-semitrailer
The longest and, generally, heaviest type of truck. The front part of the truck, containing cab and engine, is the tractor, which pulls the trailer (cargo area). Also called "tractor-trailer," "semi," or "18-wheeler." Maximum weight: 80,000 pounds (36,320 kilograms).

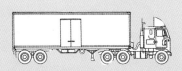

*Maximum weight according to federal **regulations** for U.S. interstate highways.

THE DIESEL ENGINE

Tractor-trailer trucks, or "semis," are the largest, heaviest trucks using the public highway systems. Most heavy trucks are powered by a **diesel engine** rather than the standard gasoline engine. Both types of engines are versions of the **internal-combustion engine.**

The diesel engine was invented by a German engineer named Rudolf Diesel. In the 1880's, Diesel became aware of the work being done by Gottlieb Daimler and others to develop the internal-combustion engine. Diesel set out to create a more efficient and powerful engine that would ignite the fuel simply with high heat. In 1897, Diesel demonstrated his first successful compression-ignition engine. The new engine was an immediate success.

The diesel engine

Like gasoline engines, diesel engines commonly use the four-stroke combustion cycle, but they burn fuel without spark plugs, using intense pressure instead.

How it works

All types of internal-combustion engines release energy from fuel by causing a continuous chain of tiny explosions in piston-fitted cylinders. The motion of the pistons turns a crankshaft, which delivers power through a transmission to the wheels. In the gasoline-powered engine of a car, the explosions are continuously ignited by sparks from spark plugs.

The diesel engine, by contrast, ignites fuel without the need for spark plugs. Instead, such intense pressure is created in the **combustion** chambers that the air-fuel mixture ignites simply

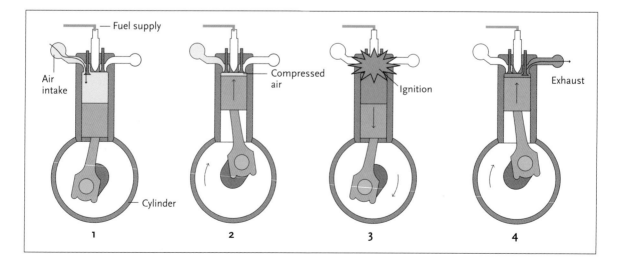

from the high heat. (Pressurizing air raises its temperature.) The pressure in a diesel combustion chamber may be twice that of a standard gasoline engine, and temperatures may reach 4500 °F (2480 °C).

Diesel pollution

Diesel engines provide greater power and are more efficient than gasoline engines. They are used not only in large trucks but also in train **locomotives**, ship engines, buses, bulldozers, and other heavy equipment. However, diesel engines produce more pollution than gasoline engines.

Like the gasoline engine, the diesel engine releases **exhaust** from compression chambers after burning fuel. This exhaust is continually conducted to the outside of the truck, releasing polluting emissions into the atmosphere. The **Environmental Protection Agency (EPA)**, the federal agency that works to protect the U.S. environment from pollution, has classified diesel exhaust as a potential human carcinogen—that is, diesel exhaust may cause cancer.

Diesel emissions include **carbon dioxide**, the main cause of **global warming;** carbon monoxide; hydrocarbons; nitrogen oxides; particulates; and other **pollutants.** (For a description of these substances and their effects, see the chart on page 10.) Diesel emissions also include the highly toxic sulfur dioxide. Sulfur dioxide and nitrogen oxides contribute to the formation of smog and **acid rain.** Particulates irritate the eyes, nose, throat, and lungs.

Compared to gasoline engines, diesel engines are more polluting. Diesel vehicles account for only 12 percent of highway miles driven in the United States, but they contribute nearly half of the nitrogen oxide pollutants. They also contribute more than two-thirds of the particulate matter among all transportation sources.

Rudolf Diesel was a German engineer who introduced the diesel engine in 1897.

Higher-grade diesel fuel releases fewer pollutants than standard diesel.

MAKING DIESEL GREEN

Diesel engines run on a special type of fuel called diesel fuel. Traditionally, most diesel engines have used **petrodiesel**, diesel-grade fuel refined from **petroleum**. Today, some truckers are using **biodiesel** or blends made of petrodiesel mixed with biodiesel.

In the United States, federal laws now require petroleum refineries to produce much cleaner diesel fuel than in the past. Diesel fuel typically contains lots of sulfur, which combines with oxygen in air to produce toxic sulfur dioxide. A grade of diesel fuel called Low Sulfur Diesel (LSD) contains about 500 parts per million (ppm) of sulfur. It will be completely phased out by 2010. Ultra Low Sulfur Diesel (ULSD) fuel, which contains 15 ppm of sulfur, is replacing LSD fuel. All new diesel vehicles manufactured in 2007 and later must be designed to use only ULSD.

The chart below lists green features being incorporated into today's new diesel vehicles.

Pollution-control and Fuel-economy Features for Diesel Vehicles	
Feature	Description
Diesel oxidation catalyst (DOC)	Same as the **catalytic converter** in a car; reduces carbon monoxide, hydrocarbon, and particulate emissions.
Diesel particulate matter filters	Ceramic devices that collect particulates in the exhaust stream.
Selective catalytic reduction (SCR) device	A variation of the catalytic converter; reduces nitrogen oxide pollutants especially.
Automatic engine **idle** device	Automatically shuts down the engine when not in use.
Improved aerodynamic designs	Designing an aerodynamic shape (instead of a boxy shape) for a large truck reduces drag caused by friction with air and increases **fuel efficiency.**
Low-rolling resistance tires	Rolling resistance describes how much the engine must work to overcome friction with the road surface in order to move the truck. Low-rolling resistance tires reduce this work and improve fuel efficiency.
Auto-tire-inflation systems (ATIS)	Trucks, like cars, get the best mileage when tires are inflated properly. The ATIS uses a microprocessor to control and regulate tire pressure.

The problem of retrofitting

New trucks are being manufactured with state-of-the art pollution control and fuel-efficiency features. However, many trucks provide up to 30 years service on the highways. We may not benefit fully from current improvements in technology for many years unless older trucks are taken in for **retrofitting**. Retrofitting is the process of adding new features to older machines or devices.

It is costly to retrofit. Many truckers and trucking companies are struggling under the burden of higher and higher prices for petrodiesel. Experts argue that government assistance will be needed to achieve widespread conversion of older trucks to newer technology. The state of California, which has for many years been a leader in fighting transportation-related pollution, has an assistance plan called the Carl Moyer program. This program provides annual grants to retrofit older California trucks with newer technology. A number of senators and representatives in the U.S. Congress support the creation of a federal assistance plan for truckers and trucking companies.

Biodiesel

Biodiesel is a type of **biofuel** that can be made from many types of oil-bearing plants. In Germany, the leading biodiesel-producing country, most biodiesel is made from canola oil. Most biodiesel in the United States is made from soybean oil. Biodiesel can even be made from leftover cooking oil from restaurants.

Biodiesel burns much more cleanly than petrodiesel, and it is made from **renewable resources**. The main drawback is that it is not widely available. Getting biodiesel to the pump in large quantities is a major challenge for the energy industry.

Soybeans can be turned into biodiesel, which burns much cleaner than traditional diesel.

Buses

Section Summary

Buses are the most common form of public transportation in many countries. Like trucks and other heavy forms of transportation, buses run on diesel fuel, which burns less cleanly than gasoline. Making buses more fuel efficient and reducing their harmful emissions are major focuses of governments and environmental groups.

Some buses have been designed to run on natural gas. Others use fuel-cell batteries, which use hydrogen gas to power them. Hybrid buses, which use batteries along with a diesel-powered engine, are also available. All of these alternatives release fewer pollutants than standard buses.

In the United States and elsewhere, buses are the most common form of **mass transit.** Buying and maintaining a fleet of transit buses costs considerably less than building a train system in an **urban** area. Buses are also used to transport children to school and to carry passengers between cities.

Millions of children take buses to school, but some buses are extremely polluting.

Like other heavy forms of transportation, buses rely largely on diesel power. Diesel fuel burns less cleanly than gasoline in cars. Improving the **fuel efficiency** and **emissions** profile of buses is a major focus of governments and environmental groups.

School buses

In the United States, about 24 million children go to school on school buses every day. Most of these buses are powered by **diesel engines.** Some school districts are using buses that are 30 years old or older. These older diesel buses are particularly polluting. In fact, buses manufactured before the 1990 model year have few or no emissions-control features.

These high-emissions diesel school buses contribute significantly to pollution in the atmosphere and put their riders at risk of high exposure to diesel **pollutants.** According to one study published in 2005, children riding on 30-year-old buses inhaled 70 percent more pollutants than passengers riding in cars.

The problem is complicated by the fact that many U.S. public school districts operate under serious budget restrictions. Replacing outmoded buses with new, cleaner alternatives will likely require help from the federal government and states.

Green buses

As with other forms of transportation, engineers and scientists the world over are conducting research to develop less polluting buses. **Hybrid** buses are being added to mass transit systems in many cities around the United States, Canada, and Europe. These vehicles operate on the same principles as hybrid cars, combining diesel engines with electric motors and batteries.

Some bus companies and public transportation systems are also beginning to use **biofuels.** Typically, biofuels for buses are used in blends with **petrodiesel,** often as B10 or B20 blends.

Some buses, like their counterparts among cars, have been designed to run on natural gas. Natural gas buses are far less polluting than diesel buses. However, the system of fuel stations for **natural gas vehicles** is not yet well developed.

Hydrogen **fuel cell** buses make up a small part of several European mass transit systems, and are starting to appear in some U.S. cities. Like fuel cell cars, these buses use hydrogen gas as fuel and produce no **exhaust** or pollutants. In 2006, Oakland, California, became the first U.S. city to add hydrogen-powered buses to its public transportation system.

Many cities around the world are adding hybrid buses to their fleets.

Trains

Section Summary

Trains provide transportation for people and heavy goods across long distances. Most trains that transport goods include a locomotive with a diesel engine. This engine is powered by a petroleum-based fuel called petrodiesel. Trains burn a lot of fuel and are responsible for releasing harmful pollutants to the air.

Hybrid trains use a diesel locomotive engine along with electric motors powered by batteries. A few trains now use biodiesel blends, which burn cleaner than petrodiesel. Perhaps the most promising technology is that of magnetic levitation trains (maglevs), which are emissions-free.

Trains are connected lines of vehicles that move along rails or other specialized roadways. Railroads provide the most inexpensive method of land transportation over long distances.

Two major categories of trains are **freight** trains, which haul heavy cargo, and passenger trains, which move people within cities, from city to city, and even across continents.

Freight trains

Freight trains are made up of various types of cars and typically haul bulk goods, such as chemicals, coal, grain, iron ore, and **petroleum**. They also carry manufactured goods, such as automobiles and machinery. Refrigerated cars on trains enable them to carry perishable foods, such as meat.

Freight trains powered by diesel locomotives can weigh more than 20,000 tons (18,100 metric tons).

Freight trains and many passenger trains are pulled on tracks by **locomotives.** Most locomotives used for heavy work are powered by **diesel engines** burning **petrodiesel** fuel. Like other types of diesel engines, locomotives send out polluting **emissions** into the air. This airborne mix includes **carbon dioxide**, carbon monoxide, hydrocarbons, nitrogen oxides, sulfur dioxide, **particulates**, and other **pollutants.**

Locomotive pollution tends to become concentrated in major rail hubs. In Chicago, the busiest U.S. rail hub, locomotives annually emit as much nitrogen oxide pollution as 25 million new cars, according to the Environmental Defense Fund, a U.S. environmental group. Other major U.S. rail hubs, such as Los Angeles, Houston-Galveston, Dallas-Fort Worth, Baltimore, and Detroit, also have high locomotive pollution levels.

New technologies

Scientists and engineers are researching ways to reduce diesel emissions from switcher locomotives, which are used in rail yards to sort cars and build trains. Switchers locomotives perform tasks that involve a lot of starting and stopping, which is less fuel efficient than traveling long distances at the same speed.

Hybrid switcher locomotives use battery power that is backed up by off-highway diesel engines, which are more fuel efficient than standard diesel engines. These engines provide power only when the batteries need to be recharged.

Some switcher locomotives are also used for short trips, which require high speed and lots of power. Since the amount of power needed by these locomotives varies, engineers have designed multi-engine switcher locomotives, which use the number of engines needed for a particular task. For example, all engines in a switcher locomotive may be needed on a short-distance trip, but only one engine may be needed for work around the rail yard. According to Railpower, a Canadian-based company that manufactures hybrid and multi-engine switcher locomotives, hybrid and multi-engine technologies reduce fuel consumption by up to 60 percent and emissions by 80 percent.

Freight trains or trucks?

Some **environmentalists** think that using more trains instead of trucks to haul freight would reduce diesel emissions. Each truck uses its own diesel engine to carry a limited amount of cargo, while freight trains consist of many cars and one or two locomotives. However, it would not be an easy task to change freight patterns in the United States—or elsewhere. Moreover, a greater concentration of locomotives in certain rail centers could create more local pollution.

Multi-engine locomotives, such as the one below, use only the number of engines they need for a particular task.

Intercity bullet trains reach high speeds, sometimes exceeding 300 miles per hour (483 kilometers per hour).

TRANSPORTING PEOPLE

Trains transport people from place to place in a wide variety of ways. Passenger trains range from short-distance railroads that haul cars by cables up steep hills to large, intercity trains that whisk passengers across whole countries. Specialized kinds of trains also provide transportation within cities and **urban** areas.

Intercity passenger trains

Most countries have passenger train systems that provide transportation between major cities and towns. Such systems are highly developed in Western Europe and Japan. They feature **bullet trains**—passenger trains that travel extremely fast—between major cities.

Intercity passenger rail is often a greener strategy for long-distance travel than either cars or airplanes. Every car has its own engine and outputs emissions. However, on a typical passenger train, one locomotive with one diesel engine transports hundreds of people. Passenger trains also help minimize traffic **congestion** by reducing the number of cars on crowded roads and highways.

Passenger rail could offer some relief to the world's overburdened airlines. However, creating the **infrastructure** for a modernized passenger rail system is expensive. In the United States, passenger rail has received little government support for many years. To update the U.S. system to match systems in Germany, France, or Japan would require huge investments. However, the environmental payoff might be great.

Passenger trains can be much lighter in weight than freight

trains. For this reason, a variety of new green technologies are being developed for use in passenger train systems.

Hybrid trains

In July 2007, Japan introduced a hybrid-powered passenger train into its extensive passenger train system. The train has a diesel locomotive engine, but each car is equipped with electric motors powered by batteries. When a surge of power is needed—to climb a hill, for example—the diesel engine kicks in. The electric motors also use **regenerative braking** to recharge the batteries. An onboard computer coordinates the use of diesel and electric power, as well as the recharging phase.

Biodiesel trains

Biodiesel trains are also in the early stages of development. In June 2007, the United Kingdom began using 20-percent biodiesel fuel in passenger trains running between London and Wales as a test of future conversion to biodiesel blends. As with other types of diesel engines, locomotive engines can use certain biodiesel blends without any mechanical changes but would require **retrofitting** to convert to 100-percent biodiesel.

Maglev trains

An entirely new technology for trains has been in development for some time. Magnetic levitation trains, called **maglevs**, use magnetic forces to levitate (float) a train above a specialized track called a guideway. Maglev trains are quiet and emissions-free, and they can go very fast. Also, maglev trains cause no friction because they float over the surface and do not actually touch any track. They have no moving parts. Engineers think that maglev trains would hardly ever wear out. However, maglev trains require an extremely different infrastructure from conventional trains, so they are very expensive to build.

The Shanghai Maglev Train is the world's first commercial high-speed maglev train. It began operating in January 2004.

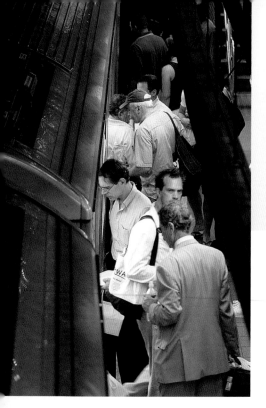

TRAINS FOR MASS TRANSIT

Trains play an important role in providing transportation within urban areas. An integrated system of trains and buses for public transportation within an urban area is called **mass transit**. Most mass transit is funded and run by city or regional urban governments. In some cases, mass transit is run by private companies but is coordinated and overseen by government agencies.

The use of trains or buses in a mass transit system is almost always a green transportation option. Most mass-transit trains are electric-powered vehicles that do not give off emissions, though they do rely on power plants for electricity. Moreover, commuter trains are capable of carrying hundreds of people at a time. By contrast, carpooling can achieve only four or five people per vehicle, and the majority of auto commuters travel with only one person in each car.

In today's world of rapidly rising fuel prices and environmental threats, mass transit is getting a lot of consideration in cities across North America and around the world. Several kinds of trains are used in urban mass transit systems. Some are listed in the chart below.

More than six million commuters use New York City's subway system each weekday.

Kinds of Trains Used in Mass Transit	
Kind of train	Description
Commuter train	Large-capacity train, usually diesel-powered, that travels between a city center and its suburbs; used mostly by commuters going to and from work.
Heavy rail	Electric railway with a capacity for heavy traffic volume; can run on elevated tracks or in subways in a city.
Light rail	Lightweight passenger rail cars operating on a fixed railway that may or may not be completely separated from ground traffic; electric power is provided either by an overhead electric line or through the rails.
Aerial tramway	A short-route electric system of aerial cables with suspended passenger vehicles.

Vancouver's SkyTrain

Greater Vancouver is Canada's third largest metropolitan area, and it is growing rapidly. It is also home to one of the most advanced light-rail systems in North America.

In preparation for hosting Expo 86, a world's fair in 1986, Vancouver built and opened its light-rail starter system, called SkyTrain. Additional lines have since been added, expanding the system by 30 miles (49.5 kilometers). Two new lines, one of them connecting the center city to the Vancouver International Airport in preparation for the 2010 Vancouver Winter Olympics, will further expand the system by 18 miles (30.5 kilometers). Vancouver officials have plans to add still more new lines after 2010.

SkyTrain is a fully automated, driverless system. The trains are controlled from a central facility, though attendants are usually on the trains. Vehicles carry up to 75 passengers and run in pairs at up to 50 miles per hour (80 kilometers per hour). According to British Columbia Rapid Transit, SkyTrain carries more than 65 million passengers each year.

Vancouver also has a trolley system that uses electric trolleys. These buslike vehicles have pulleys (called trolleys) that attach the vehicle to an overhead electric line for power. In 2006, Vancouver's trolley system provided about 91 million rides. With both SkyTrain and the trolley bus system, Vancouver offers ample attractive alternatives to car travel.

A CLOSER LOOK
Phoenix's Light Rail Transit

In 2000, residents of Phoenix, Arizona, approved a funding measure to build a regional light rail system. The new Phoenix Light Rail Transit (LRT) starter system, 20.3 miles (32.7 kilometers) long, began operations in late 2008. Traffic experts predicted that the light rail service could lead to a 40 percent or better reduction in rush-hour highway congestion. Phoenix officials and transportation experts have developed plans to build a northern extension to the mainly east-west line as soon as 2012 and a southern extension sometime later in the decade.

SkyTrain does not need drivers because trains are controlled from a central facility.

Ships and Boats

Diesel container ships can carry more than 100,000 tons (90,718 metric tons) of freight.

Section Summary

Ships are used mainly to transport goods, though people also use them for travel and recreation. Most ships are powered by diesel engines. Ship diesel emissions include such harmful pollutants as carbon dioxide.

In order to reduce pollution from large ships, some people are switching to fuels that are a blend of biodiesel (fuel made from plants) and petrodiesel (fuel made from petroleum).

Boats are small water vessels often used for recreation. Like ships, some boats now run on biodiesel blends. Solar-powered boats are also being developed. These vessels use solar panels to power electric motors.

People make and use water vessels of all sizes and weights, from kayaks and small rowboats to oil supertankers and ocean luxury liners that carry hundreds of passengers.

Ships are large water vessels that mainly carry goods, though some are used to transport passengers for travel and recreation. For thousands of years, ships were powered in two ways: by sails that took advantage of wind power; and by human power provided by rowers. During the 1800's, steam-powered ships became common. These ships were usually fueled by coal. Around 100 years ago, most **commercial** ships were converted to diesel power, and today diesel remains the power source for the great majority of ships.

A ship's engine

The cargo ship pictured on this page is a modern container ship. Large container ships measure more than 1,000 feet (305 meters) in length, and they weigh millions of pounds when loaded. Moving such a massive object requires a very powerful engine with intense energy input.

A large ship engine is a **diesel engine** with a few modifications. Instead of driving a crankshaft, the up-and-down piston movement turns a long rod connected to a propeller in the water just behind the ship. This rod, called the propeller shaft, causes the propeller to spin rapidly in water, moving the ship forward.

Ship diesel emissions

A diesel ship engine is much more efficient than a gasoline engine in a car or a diesel engine in a truck. Nonetheless, the diesel engine of a large container ship under full power can consume as much as 1,660 gallons (6,283 liters) of diesel fuel every hour. Ship diesel **emissions** include many harmful **pollutants**, such as **carbon dioxide**, nitrogen oxides, sulfur dioxide, **particulates**, and other substances.

In the United States, large, diesel-powered oceangoing ships dock at ports on or near the Pacific coast, the Gulf coast, and the Atlantic coast. According to environmental groups, a large container ship coming into port can release as much harmful air pollution as a diesel truck making three trips around Earth. Medical studies have demonstrated the harmful effects of these diesel emissions on the health of people living near port facilities.

A large cargo ship consumes more energy than many green technologies can deliver. Cleaner power alternatives for very large ships may not be available in the near future, so ship designers maximize technology to promote energy efficiency.

Smaller ships and boats

Not all water vessels are mammoth cargo carriers. Many smaller-scale ships and boats are used for a variety of purposes. Boats are powered by either a gasoline or diesel engine.

Passenger boats, such as harbor cruise boats and small ferries, are good candidates for using alternate energy sources. These sources include wind power, **solar power**, and **biodiesel** fuels.

In 2004, the port at Houston, Texas, was rated the most polluted port in the United States.

A CLOSER LOOK
Dirty Ports

In 2004, the Natural Resources Defense Council, a New York City-based environmental organization, released a "report card" on environmental quality at and near ports. Among the 10 busiest U.S. container ship ports, grades ranged from B-minus down to F, with Oakland, California, getting the best score and Houston, Texas, the worst. The bustling Los Angeles-Long Beach port complex is the largest single source of air pollution in all of southern California.

In 2008, the U.S. Congress held hearings on pollution affecting the nation's ports. Legislators called the hearings in response to charges that the chief cause of severe port pollution was a lack of governmental **regulation**.

Many smaller ships and boats, such as these research vessels for the Great Lakes Environmental Research Laboratory in Michigan, can run on biofuels.

BIODIESEL POWER

Biofuels are liquid fuels made from living things or their products. One type of biofuel is biodiesel, typically made from oil-bearing plants, such as soybeans. Biodiesel has many advantages over **petrodiesel** (diesel made from **petroleum**). It is made from **renewable resources** and gives off less harmful emissions than petrodiesel. Also, biodiesel is far less toxic than petroleum, so accidental spills are less damaging to bodies of water.

Biodiesel blends

As with cars and trucks, biodiesel is being used as ship fuel mainly in the form of blends. Even some large cargo ships are using B20, a blend of 20 percent biodiesel and 80 percent petrodiesel. Biodiesel blends reduce emissions without requiring major changes to the engine. Some experts in marine technology caution that we are unlikely to have large ships powered solely by biodiesel any time soon. This is because biodiesel is less dense with energy than petrodiesel, so more would have to be carried in fuel tanks, adding weight to the ship and reducing cargo space.

Going green with biodiesel

Today, many boat owners and operators are taking a serious look at biodiesel, particularly B20, which is the most widely available biodiesel fuel. In 2008, the Washington State Department of

Transportation began phasing in the use of B20 fuel to power ferries operating in Puget Sound. The action was in response to an executive order issued by Washington Governor Christine Gregoire for state agencies to adopt **sustainable** fuel practices.

Earthrace

In 2006, the first 100-percent biodiesel-powered boat set sail in New Zealand. Designed by oil industry engineer Peter Bethune, *Earthrace* can master both calm seas and rough waters, cruising at speeds of up to 45 knots (52 miles per hour/83 kilometers per hour). The boat's fuel tank holds 2,500 gallons (9,463 liters), which gives *Earthrace* a range of 3,000 miles (4,826 kilometers) between visits to fuel pumps.

To enhance his biodiesel-powered vessel, Bethune adopted an unusual design. Most boats have one hull—the outer body of a ship. *Earthrace,* however, is a multi-hulled boat consisting of one central hull and two outlying hulls, all connected by crossbeams. This design derives from large canoes crafted and used by Polynesian people long ago. *Earthrace* also has a long, pointed bow (front end), which allows it to pierce through and briefly dive under waves.

Earthrace was launched on February 24, 2006, in New Zealand. Later in 2006, Bethune and his crew embarked on a promotional tour to showcase biodiesel water transportation. The tour became a major media event in U.S. cities that were visited, such as Seattle, as well as other cities around the world. Visits to a number of ports allowed the team to spread the word about biodiesel. Bethune and his crew also intended to challenge the standing record for circumnavigation of the globe by a powerboat. By piercing through waves, *Earthrace* can maintain a higher overall speed—all while setting new standards in boating green.

Earthrace's unusual hull allows it to pierce through waves, saving fuel.

Robert Dane's solar sailboat design utilizes solar and wind energy and is emissions-free.

SOLAR-SAIL POWER

In the late 1990's, an Australian doctor named Robert Dane sought to make a new kind of boat by modifying the wing sails he had seen on racing boats. A wing sail is a semi-rigid sail that functions similarly to an airplane wing, producing **lift** and increasing the power of the sails. Dane wanted to cover wing sails with **solar panels** that would allow a boat to use both sun and wind energy. The wing sail could be moved—by computer-assisted electronics—to capture sunlight or wind, allowing it to adapt to weather conditions. When strong winds threatened to destabilize the boat, the sails could be folded onto the boat's roof.

Solar-sail technology

Robert Dane's solar sailboat is an example of the recent advances made in solar-powered water transportation. Using solar and wind power requires no fuel and releases no polluting emissions into the air. However, solar power alone does not provide enough dependable power to drive commercial boats or other ships on a strict schedule. For this reason, many of the solar-powered boats being designed today are **hybrids**. These vessels have a small, on-board diesel engine to provide backup power. Operators of such boats report that they use only about one-tenth of the diesel fuel required by standard diesel-powered boats.

Storing energy from wind and sunlight is one of the chief challenges in solar-sail technology today. If researchers can find a way to efficiently store this energy, boats without any diesel backup may become more practical.

Across the Atlantic

On May 8, 2007, an odd-looking boat silently glided into the harbor of New York City. The arrival might have gone unnoticed, except that it marked a major milestone in the history of water travel. The 46-foot (14-meter) boat, a modified catamaran (a two-hulled boat) called *Sun21,* had just completed a crossing of the Atlantic Ocean from Europe to New York on solar power alone.

Sun21 was brainchild of Swiss designer Mark Wust, who worked closely with the Swiss boat-manufacturing company, MW-Line SA. Wust and his assistants took a basic catamaran design and added a roof loaded with electric-power-generating **solar cells**, which convert energy in sunlight to electrical power, and two electric motors to use the solar-generated electrical power. The motors are capable of driving the boat at up to 7 knots (8 miles per hour/13 kilometers per hour) of speed.

Wust, along with the boat's captain and three other crew members, launched *Sun21* from Basel, Switzerland, in December 2006. They rode down European canals and rivers to the North Sea in the Netherlands; then down the European coast to Spain and the Canary Islands; then across the Atlantic Ocean to the Caribbean island of Martinique; and finally up the eastern coastline to New York City. On its journey, the *Sun21* generated worldwide interest in building more solar-powered boats.

Engineers calculate that the *Sun21*'s journey would have burned 988 gallons (3,744 liters) of diesel fuel.

Airplanes

Section Summary

Airplane travel has increased dramatically over the past 50 years, causing this form of transportation to become a significant source of pollution.

Many of the alternate fuel and power sources that can be used for cars or trucks are not appropriate for large jets. However, biofuels, battery power, and other technologies may be used for smaller aircraft. They may also be used as secondary power on large jets. New designs for airplanes may also cut down on their fuel use.

An airplane is an engine-driven machine that flies through the air supported by the flow of air around its wings. As the plane moves forward on the runway, air moves faster and faster over and under the wing. The airplane wing has a shape called an airfoil, which pushes the air moving above the wing upward, creating an area of low pressure above the wing. At the same time, air moving below the wing maintains higher pressure. This difference in air pressure above and below the wing eventually becomes great enough to force the airplane off the ground.

In physics, *lift* is a term describing the force created around an airplane wing by air in motion. Lift is the reason why most airplanes must speed down a long runway to achieve

Large jets are important in global transportation, but they are also quite polluting.

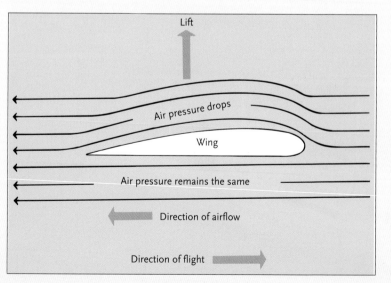

The shape of airplane wings create areas of low pressure above the wing's surface.

flight. It also explains why flying is an energy-intensive activity. The heavier the airplane, the more energy must be expended for lift to overcome gravity so that the craft can fly.

Jet engines and propellers

The term *airplane* applies both to aircraft driven by jet engines and those driven by propellers. Jet engines suck in air, ignite fuel, and spew out burned gases. The force of the escaping gases drives the jet forward. Most large **commercial** planes—which can carry hundreds of passengers—are jets. Many small planes achieve flight through the use of propellers and a single engine. The rapidly spinning propellers pull the plane foward, allowing it to gain enough speed for its wings to lift it off the ground.

Aviation

"Aviation" describes all the activities related to building and flying planes. Aviation is one of the world's largest industries. A major part of aviation is the commercial airlines that fly tens of thousands of planes every day, crisscrossing the globe.

In the early 1900's, most of the world's long-distance travelers used trains, buses, or ships. But after the development of large commercial jet airplanes in the 1950's, people could travel across the world in a matter of days. Today, such a trip may take less than a day. As the aviation industry grew around the world, airplanes quickly became one of the most important means of transportation.

Most of the world's airplanes, and all of its big commercial airplanes, run on fuel made from **petroleum.** Airplanes and jets produce much the same pollution as cars, trucks, and **freight** trains. However, jets dump much of their pollution into the upper **atmosphere**, where it may pose special dangers to the environment.

Unfortunately, alternative fuels and power sources are not well suited to commercial planes. The expanding use of energy-intensive air transportation poses a major challenge to devising greener means of global transportation.

The number of U.S. commercial airline passengers has increased dramatically over the past 50 years.

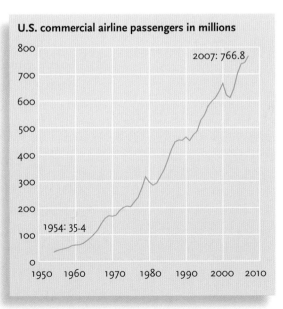

U.S. commercial airline passengers in millions

2007: 766.8

1954: 35.4

Airplanes   47

AIR TRAVEL AND POLLUTION

The number of planes flying and the number of passengers on those planes grow every year. As a result, the aviation industry is attracting much attention today from government leaders and **environmentalists.**

Airplanes release pollutants high in the atmosphere, where they may cause more harm than pollutants released on the ground.

Carbon pollution

Air transportation is adding significantly to **carbon dioxide** build-up in the atmosphere. The rising concentration of carbon dioxide is the main cause of **global warming**, according to nearly all scientists. Because the number of flights and passengers is increasing so steadily, the impact of aircraft-caused pollution is growing. Environmental scientists report that in 1990, aircraft contributed about 2.1 percent of all carbon dioxide pollution in the atmosphere. By 2008, that percentage had risen to 3 percent, and scientists project that by 2050, aircraft may be responsible for 5 percent of all carbon dioxide pollution.

High in the sky

Unlike other forms of transportation, airplanes spew their **pollutants** high in the atmosphere. Today, a standard long-distance commercial jet achieves a height of up to 8 miles (13 kilometers). Scientists believe that carbon dioxide and other components of engine **emissions** released at that height may impact the atmosphere differently from pollutants released on the ground, and they may intensify global warming. However, more scientific study is needed to understand upper-atmosphere effects.

Large commercial jets

Today, large fleets of commercial jets flying for various airlines crisscross the world. The global economy is highly dependent on high-volume air travel. Most jets flying the longer routes are large vessels capable of carrying between 200 and 500 or more passengers. These jets rely on petroleum-derived jet fuel for the tremendous energy they need to get and stay airborne.

Many of the green technologies that can be applied to cars or trucks are not appropriate for large jets. For example, **solar power** and battery power cannot deliver enough energy to power a jet. Many experts doubt that **fuel cells** could deliver enough energy. Some experts also think that **biofuels** may not be a solution. Because **ethanol** and **biodiesel** are less densely packed with energy than petroleum fuel, a jet airplane would have to be larger and heavier to hold enough of these fuels. However, research into new types of biofuel may solve this problem.

Strategies to reduce large-jet pollution

As there may not be a good alternative to petroleum-based jet fuel in the near future, many aviation experts are looking for ways to make the jet airplane more efficient. The chart below lists ideas to improve jet efficiency.

Making Commercial Jets "Leaner and Meaner"	
Concept	Description
Designing more efficient jet engines	The National Aeronautics and Space Administration is working with airplane manufacturers to develop jet engine technology that would burn 25 percent less fuel and cut nitrogen oxide emissions by 80 percent.
Using composites instead of metals in airplanes	Composites weigh far less than such metals as steel, so they can contribute to reducing fuel use.
Using global positioning system (GPS) for routing planes	Experts estimate that using GPS instead of land-based radar for air-traffic control would allow planes to fly more efficient routes, saving fuel.
Towing aircraft to runway	Jet planes waste a lot of fuel traveling from the terminal to the runway; towing airplanes to their runway lineup would save this fuel.
Changing body shape of jets	The most promising proposal is a redesigned airplane configuration called blended wing body (BWB). This design transforms the entire airplane into a huge, triangle-shaped wing.

A CLOSER LOOK
Contrails

Contrails are artificial clouds that form from the exhaust gases of jets at very cold temperatures high in the atmosphere. They often form white streaks across the sky that soon vanish. However, when conditions are right—especially when the air is humid—the contrails can grow and spread into high clouds. Because there are so many jets flying daily, many contrail clouds form. Scientists believe that contrails affect climate, but they are not yet sure how. When contrail clouds first form, they reflect sunlight back into space. In their later stages, however, they trap heat in the atmosphere.

Jet contrails

The U.S. Air Force's B-2 Spirit is probably the best-known blended wing body aircraft.

INNOVATIONS IN AVIATION

Scientists and engineers today are working on a number of concepts for flying in different—and greener—ways than in the past.

Blended wing body

In the blended wing body (BWB) design, the entire airplane is one huge triangular-shaped wing, rather like a moth at rest. All of the engine parts and all of the cargo and passenger spaces are tucked under the wing so that they become part of the wing body.

The BWB design may work for large commercial jets and is expected to be 30 percent more fuel efficient than today's standard jet planes, but BWB planes are also more difficult to control. In part, this is because they do not have a tail, which helps to stabilize airplanes. The solution is to equip the plane with sophisticated computer software that keeps the plane balanced and stabilized. However, software failure could be catastrophic.

Ethanol-powered airplanes

Some green technologies have been developed for small, light planes, such as one- or two-seaters or **unmanned aerial vehicles (UAV's)**—airplanes that fly without humans aboard. For example, aviation industry experts predict that manufacturers will produce a steadily growing number of ethanol-powered small airplanes. In March 2005, Neiva Aeronautic Industry, a Brazilian aviation company, delivered the first airplane designed specifically to be fueled by ethanol. The company followed up with the production of many more small, single-seat ethanol airplanes. Some manufacturers have provided conversion kits to help owners of older small airplanes convert to ethanol.

Hydrogen fuel cells

The same fuel-cell technology that is being developed for cars and buses can also be used to power small planes. In a fuel cell, hydrogen and oxygen are combined, producing water. The chemical reaction produces electricity, a useful source of power. In February 2008, a pilot flew a single-seat airplane fueled by a hydrogen fuel cell to 3,300 feet (1,006 meters) above Ocana, Spain. The flight marked the first time that a human has flown in a fuel cell-powered airplane.

Most aviation experts think that hydrogen fuel cell technology could be used on one- or two-seater light planes or on UAV's. Some experts also think that fuel cell technology could be used for secondary power on big commercial jets—to power lights in the cabin, for example—but not for powering the jet engines.

Battery-powered airplanes

In January 2008, a French test pilot flew the first manned flight of a battery-powered airplane. The pilot operated the wood-and-fabric, single-seat airplane for 48 minutes, covering 31 miles (50 kilometers) in the southern Alps region of France.

Aviation experts say that the greatest challenge in designing battery-powered airplanes is that batteries deliver far less energy per pound of weight than **fossil fuels**. Therefore, to provide enough power for flight, a number of batteries must be used, increasing the weight of the aircraft. Continued advances in battery technology may bring battery-powered airplanes into everyday use. However, experts believe that batteries will never be able to deliver enough power for large airplanes, and they also note that the range of smaller airplanes will be somewhat limited.

Experts are testing aircraft powered by batteries (top) and fuel cells (bottom).

Governments and Transportation

Section Summary

Most national governments have agencies that set and enforce standards for products sold in their countries, such as automobiles. Setting such standards is crucial to reducing pollution from transportation.

Governments can take several actions to reduce transportation's harmful effects on the environment. These include raising fuel efficiency standards for cars, investing in new transportation technologies, and funding public transportation.

Most pollution experts emphasize that the world's pollution problems will not be solved without the active participation of governments at all levels. National governments are especially important due to their size. Also, they can find ways to cooperate with each other to reduce pollution in global forums (meetings).

Governments can set higher fuel standards for cars, thus reducing pollution.

Government action is particularly important in the arena of transportation. Manufacturing companies make and market their cars and trucks in countries around the world. Most national governments have agencies that set and enforce standards for products sold in their countries. Governments can require companies to offer more efficient, less polluting vehicles.

CAFE standards

U.S. standards to **regulate fuel efficiency** are referred to as **CAFE standards.** CAFE stands for "Corporate Average Fuel Economy," the name of a piece of legislation passed by the U.S. Congress in the 1970's. All automobile manufacturers must adhere to CAFE standards to sell their products in the United States.

The CAFE standards are not perfect. **Sport utility vehicles (SUV's)** were originally classified as light trucks and were not regulated by the standards set in the 1970's. Later, when SUV's were brought under CAFE regulation, vehicles weighing more than 8,500 pounds (3,856 kilograms) were still not included.

Setting an example

Pollution experts feel that **industrialized countries**, such as the United States, Japan, and countries of the **European Union**, can set an example for the rest of the world in establishing environmentally sound policies. Furthermore, these economically advanced countries export their technologies to less developed countries. Because green technologies may be more expensive at first, industrialized countries will probably need to **subsidize** green technologies in the developing world.

Reducing pollution in Bangkok

The story of pollution in Bangkok, Thailand, offers an example of how government action can limit pollution. Bangkok is a **megacity** in Southeast Asia. Like many Asian megacities, it has experienced rapid growth—and choking air pollution caused by automobile traffic. That pollution reached a peak in the 1990's.

After conducting a traffic study, Bangkok officials learned that 50 percent of motor vehicles in Bangkok were motorcycles, most of which had highly polluting two-stroke engines. The city government then launched a program to promote the use of cleaner, four-stroke motorcycles. They set up checkpoints to identify and fine highly polluting vehicles.

Bangkok does not have perfect air quality today, but it is much improved from the 1990's. Many other Asian cities—such as Beijing, China, and Jakarta, Indonesia—are much more polluted.

Reducing pollution from motorcycles was key to improving air quality in Bangkok, Thailand.

Higher speeds reduce travel times but waste large amounts of fuel.

WHAT GOVERNMENTS NEED TO DO

Many experts agree that government action is the most important factor in successfully confronting the world's environmental problems. The Clean Air Act, passed by the U.S. Congress in 1970, began to regulate such polluters as factories and power plants. Then, CAFE standards enacted in the 1970's began regulating automobile pollution. Between the 1970's and the present, the United States has experienced sharp reductions in many **emissions.** The 1976 U.S. government mandate (requirement) to install **catalytic converters** in automobiles led to a 95-percent reduction of carbon monoxide pollution and a 90-percent reduction of nitrogen oxide pollution in automobile emissions.

Higher automobile efficiency standards

In December 2007, the U.S. Congress raised CAFE standards for both passenger automobiles and light trucks to 35 miles per gallon (about 15 kilometers per liter) by the year 2020. Some environmental experts wanted still higher standards. They also wanted to close the loophole for large SUV's.

Lower speed limits

Speed limits on most interstates in the United States are between 55 and 75 miles per hour (89 to 113 kilometers per hour). Vehicles lose as much as 10 percent of their efficiency for every 5 miles of speed above 55 miles per hour. State governments could reduce fuel consumption by lowering speed limits.

Investment in green technologies

Corporations are reluctant to take risks, such as investing heavily in researching new technologies. That is why financial support for new technologies from governments is critical. When new technologies mature, companies eagerly adopt them, especially if governments offer incentives for using these technologies.

The U.S. federal government and other governments around the world could invest more heavily in fuel research. Automakers and consumers will stick with **petroleum**-derived gasoline unless governments provide support in developing and adopting **biofuels**.

Tax incentives

Car-buying consumers are more likely to think green if they are given an incentive (reward) to do so. In the early 2000's, the U.S. federal government created tax credits to encourage consumers to buy **hybrid** vehicles and other green vehicles.

Other governments have taxed vehicles with poor fuel efficiency in order to discourage consumers from buying these gas guzzlers. In 2008, the government of the Netherlands imposed a special tax of nearly $30,000 on Hummers, one of the heaviest, least fuel-efficient SUV's made.

Congestion charges

In 2003, London officials enacted **congestion** charges in an 8-square-mile (20.7-square-kilometer) area of the city's center. London's plan is based on a "polluter pays" principle. Larger, more polluting vehicles must pay higher charges to enter the restricted area. Many other cities are studying ways to introduce congestion charges for their central districts.

Financial support for mass transit

Mass-transit systems in **urban** areas are extremely expensive to build. However, mass-transit systems provide an attractive travel alternative to commuters, and they can greatly reduce automobile traffic in congested city areas.

The DART system, Dallas, Texas

What You Can Do

Section Summary

Individuals can help reduce pollution through the choices they make. Taking public transportation can help reduce your carbon footprint—the amount of carbon dioxide for which your actions are responsible. For times when driving is necessary, you or your family can drive in such a way as to reduce the amount of fuel your car burns.

In the near future, people may have to pay a carbon tax, called a carbon offset, if they choose a form of transportation that uses large amounts of fossil fuels.

Everyone shares responsibility for reducing pollution in general and **carbon dioxide emissions** in particular. Though governments and world leaders will have to tackle large-scale issues related to pollution and **global warming**, each individual can take steps personally to reduce his or her **carbon footprint** (the amount of carbon dioxide an individual's actions are responsible for releasing into the air).

Individual choices, such as choosing to drive an electric car, can make a big impact.

Eco-driving

In the United States, most people need to use cars at one time or another, but the way in which people drive and maintain their cars can have a large effect on the consumption of fuel and output of emissions. The "Closer Look" sidebar on page 57 lists recommendations for becoming an "eco-friendly" driver.

Transportation choices

Many of us have a variety of transportation options that we do not use as often as we could. Walking and bicycling are always green alternatives to driving a car. Whenever possible, choose one of these self-powered, healthy transportation options. If you live in an **urban** area with available public transportation, use it.

Carbon offsets

Soon, people the world over may be required to purchase **carbon offsets** to use a particularly dirty technology—such as driving a large car with low **fuel efficiency** or taking lots of trips by jet. Here is how such a system, called **cap and trade**, would work: Each business and individual would receive a certain number of carbon credits. They would then make choices about how much fuel, electric power, heating oil, or other **carbon-dioxide**-producing products and services to use. People or businesses that **conserve** energy and have credits left over would be able to sell them to consumers that use more energy.

A cap-and-trade system has already greatly reduced pollution from sulfur dioxide, which causes **acid rain.** In 1990, the U.S. government established a cap-and-trade system for sulfur dioxide. Experts agree that the system has been a great success. Levels of sulfur dioxide have fallen even faster than expected, and the program has cost considerably less than projected. The big advantage of cap and trade is that it gives people financial incentives to become greener. By making smart investments, we can restore Earth's natural balance.

A CLOSER LOOK
What You Can Do

- Check your tires frequently. Improperly inflated tires reduce **fuel economy.**
- Use air conditioning only when it is most needed. Air conditioning uses a lot of fuel.
- Stick to the posted speed limits. Remember that driving over 55 miles per hour (89 kilometers per hour) reduces fuel economy.
- Use cruise control when driving on the open highway. It saves fuel.
- When possible, accelerate evenly, not in jerks. Avoid sudden braking.
- Keep your car maintained properly. Poorly operating car engines give off more emissions than properly maintained engines.
- Park "smart." On hot days, try to park in the shade. If you cannot find shade, use windshield shades to reduce the build-up of heat inside the vehicle. This will reduce the need for air conditioning.
- When buying a car, choose a fuel-efficient model. Do not buy a car larger than you need. In today's market, most hybrid automobiles are an eco-friendly choice. But be sure to check fuel efficiency—a hybrid sport utility vehicle may not be very efficient overall.

Riding a bicycle is always a green choice—and it can help you stay fit, too.

Activities

MAKE AN ECO-DRIVING BOOKLET

Introduction

Taking public transportation, walking, and riding a bike are easy ways to reduce **carbon dioxide emissions** caused by transportation, but many people live in areas where driving a car is sometimes necessary. Keeping up with car maintenance and "eco-driving"—driving in such a way as to increase **fuel economy**—are ways in which all drivers can reduce their **carbon footprint.** You can make an eco-driving booklet to share such tips with family and friends.

Choosing small, fuel-efficient vehicles and practicing eco-driving can help reduce carbon dioxide emissions.

Materials

- Several sheets of blank paper
- Stapler
- Pen or marker

Directions:

1. Research information about eco-driving. You can include information from page 57 of this book. You can also look up additional information on the Internet or at your library. The following Web sites include tips on eco-driving:

United States Environmental Protection Agency Tips for Driving the Smart Way
http://www.epa.gov/smartway/consumer/tips.htm

Canada's Office of Energy Efficiency
http://oee.nrcan.gc.ca/transportation/personal/driving.cfm?attr=8

World Wildlife Fund-Australia Eco-driving Tips
http://www.wwf.org.au/act/takeaction/eco-driving-tips

2. Once you have information on eco-driving, create your booklet. Turn the sheets of paper so they are horizontal and then fold them in half. You now have two pages for each sheet of paper. Fill the pages with information on eco-driving. Remember to write text in your own words—don't copy text exactly

from the sources you use. You may also wish to include a list of the sources you used at the end of your booklet.

3. If you would like several copies of your eco-driving guide, photocopy the pages. Then staple along the fold you created in Step 1 to create the binding for your booklet. You now have an eco-driving guide to share with family and friends!

ORGANIZE AN ALTERNATIVE TRANSPORTATION DAY

Introduction
Many people have the opportunity to get places by walking, riding a bike, or taking a bus or a train but are in the habit of driving a car. Enlist friends, family, and community members to help organize an alternative transportation day.

Materials
- Poster board or blank pieces of paper
- Pens and markers

Directions:
1. Create posters and flyers to announce your alternative transportation day. These should include key information about the event, such as its purpose and the day of the event.

2. Get permission to distribute posters and flyers at your school and local businesses to create awareness of the event. You can also ask your school librarian to post information about the event on the library's Web site.

3. On the day of the event, distribute additional information about how community members can make a difference. You could distribute your booklet on eco-friendly driving (see activity on page 58). You can also include additional information, such as choices people can make when purchasing cars. If you have a blog, you can post the information there and distribute cards with your blog's URL link.

Riding a bike or taking public transportation can help reduce our impact on the environment.

Glossary

acid rain rain that has a high concentration of acids because of air pollution.

biodiesel a type of biofuel used by diesel engines.

biofuel a liquid fuel made from plant matter, animal waste, or other biological sources.

blended wing body (BWB) an airplane design that may produce greater lift and improve fuel economy in airplanes.

bullet train a passenger train that travels extremely fast between cities.

CAFE standards U.S. government standards that regulate fuel efficiency in automobiles.

cap and trade a system that creates a market in pollution credits.

carbon cycle the natural processes by which carbon circulates between the atmosphere, oceans, and all living things.

carbon dioxide a colorless, odorless gas given off by burning and by animals breathing out.

carbon footprint the total amount of carbon dioxide given off by a particular human activity.

carbon offset a credit purchased to release a certain amount of carbon dioxide.

catalytic converter a device found in cars that reduces emissions from engine exhaust.

cellulose tightly-bound chains of sugar molecules that make up cell walls in plants.

combustion burning; a chemical reaction in which oxygen combines with a fuel, giving off energy, carbon dioxide, and other by-products.

commercial having to do with trade or business.

congestion an overcrowding of cars or people.

conserve to keep from harm or loss; preserve.

crude oil the form of oil that comes directly out of the ground; petroleum.

diesel engine a type of internal-combustion engine in which ignition occurs spontaneously by introducing fuel into very hot, compressed air.

electron an extremely tiny particle in atoms that carries a negative charge.

emission an airborne waste product.

Environmental Protection Agency (EPA) the federal agency that works to protect the U.S. environment from pollution.

environmentalist a person who wants to preserve nature and reduce pollution.

ethanol a widely used biofuel made from plants or algae; ethyl alcohol.

exhaust partially burned gases, such as those given off by most automobiles when they are running.

European Union (EU) an economic and political organization that includes most of the countries of Europe.

fertilizer a substance that helps plants to grow.

fossil fuel underground deposits that were formed millions of years ago from the remains of plants and animals. Coal, oil, and natural gas are fossil fuels.

freight goods carried by a form of transportation.

fuel cell an energy-producing device in which a chemical reaction takes place between hydrogen and oxygen, producing energy and water.

fuel economy the overall efficiency of a vehicle, which is affected by weight, size, engine type, driving habits, and other factors.

fuel efficiency the proportion of energy released by fuel combustion that is converted into useful energy.

global warming the gradual warming of Earth's

surface, believed to be caused by a build-up of greenhouse gases in the atmosphere.

greenhouse effect the process by which certain gases cause the Earth's atmosphere to warm.

greenhouse gas any gas that contributes to the greenhouse effect.

gyroscope a device that uses rotation to produce a stable orientation.

herbicide a poison that kills weeds.

hybrid a vehicle in which power can be produced by either batteries or by a gasoline-powered engine.

idle to run slowly without transmitting power; a motor idles when it runs slowly, out of gear.

industrialized country a country where historical wealth and advanced development contribute to a relatively high standard of living.

infrastructure roads, bridges, buildings, and other public facilities.

internal-combustion engine a type of engine used widely in cars that creates power through continual, tiny explosions in piston-fitted cylinders.

lift the force created around an airplane wing by its motion through the air; the force which lifts an airplane off the ground.

locomotive a railway vehicle that contains an engine, which provides power for a train.

maglev a technology for train propulsion in which electromagnets are used to levitate the train and push or pull it along a specialized guideway.

mass transit an integrated system of trains and buses for public transportation within a city or urban area.

megacity an urban area with 10 million or more residents.

natural gas vehicle (NGV) a vehicle that uses natural gas as fuel.

nonrenewable resources resources that cannot be replenished once depleted, such as fossil fuels.

ozone a form of oxygen gas.

particulate a tiny piece of solid material that floats in the air.

petrodiesel diesel-grade fuel refined from crude oil.

petroleum another name for the fossil fuel often called oil.

pollutant a single source of pollution.

regenerative braking the process of capturing energy from normal braking to recharge batteries.

regulate; regulation control by rule, principle, or system.

renewable resource natural resources, such as trees, that can be replaced after they have been harvested.

retrofitting the process of adding new features to older machines or devices.

rush hour times of the day when workers are traveling to work or home from work.

smog a brown, hazy mixture of gases and particulates caused by exhaust gases released by automobiles and other users of fossil fuels.

solar cell a tiny device that converts the energy in sunlight to electric current.

solar panel a panel of solar cells.

solar power electric power that is created from the energy in sunlight.

sport utility vehicle (SUV) a passenger vehicle that combines the features of a station wagon and a truck.

subsidize to aid or assist with a grant of money or by guaranteeing a market.

unmanned aerial vehicle (UAV) an airplane that flies without any humans aboard.

urban of or related to cities.

zero emissions vehicle (ZEV) a vehicle that produces no emissions; typically applicable to battery-powered motorcycles.

Additional Resources

WEB SITES

AIRNow

http://www.airnow.gov

A government-backed program that offers much information about pollution; includes a student page, "Kid's Air."

Air Pollution: What's the Solution?

http://www.ciese.org/curriculum/airproj

An educational project for grades K-12.

Environment Agency

http://www.environmentagency.gov.uk/
subjects/airquality/?lang=_e

The "Air quality" page provides ways people in the United Kingdom are helping to make the air cleaner; includes resources for schools.

Environmental Working Group

http://www.ewg.org

Much information about pollution and the environment.

Envirolink

http://www.envirolink.org

A nonprofit that provides access to thousands of online environmental resources.

Friends of the Earth: Transport

http://www.foe.co.uk/campaigns/transport/
index.html

Inspires solutions to help the United Kingdom reverse the pollution caused by transportation.

Scorecard

http://www.scorecard.org

Answers to common inquiries on nationwide pollution in the United States.

United States Department of Energy: Alternative & Advanced Fuels

http://www.eere.energy.gov/afdc/fuels/index.html

Discusses about a dozen fuels that could serve as energy sources for vehicles.

World News: Pollution

http://www.wn.com/pollution

Contains lots of pollution information in an easily navigable format.

BOOKS

Air Pollution: Problems and Solutions
by J. S. and Renee A. Kidd (Facts on File, 2006)

Alternative Cars
by Jill C. Wheeler (ABDO, 2008)

Endangered Planet
by David Burnie (Kingfisher, 2004)

**Energy Alternatives:
Opposing Viewpoints**
by Laura S. Friedman (Greenhaven, 2006)

Global Pollution
by Paul Brown (Raintree, 2003)

Pollution: Opposing Viewpoints
edited by Louise I. Gerdes (Greenhaven, 2006)

Pollution
by Louise I. Gerdes, ed. (Greenhaven 2006)

Pollution
by Clive Gifford (Heinemann Library, 2006)

Pollution A to Z
by Richard M. Stapleton, ed. (Macmillan Reference, 2004)

Index